BROTHERTON PO

Brotherton Poetry Prize Anthology

2019

PRESENTED BY THE
UNIVERSITY OF LEEDS
POETRY CENTRE

judged by
SIMON ARMITAGE, MALIKA BOOKER,
MELVYN BRAGG, STELLA BUTLER,
VAHNI CAPILDEO & JOHN WHALE

with an introduction by
SIMON ARMITAGE

CARCANET

First published in Great Britain in 2020 by
Carcanet
Alliance House, 30 Cross Street
Manchester M2 7AQ
www.carcanet.co.uk

A CIP catalogue record for this book is
available from the British Library.
ISBN 978 1 78410 923 3

Book design by Andrew Latimer
Printed in Great Britain by SRP Ltd, Exeter, Devon

The publisher acknowledges financial
assistance from Arts Council England.

CONTENTS

ABOUT THE PRIZE

The University of Leeds has a proud tradition of supporting new poetry and of exploring the poetry of the past. Geoffrey Hill was a member of staff from 1954 to 1978 and Leeds alumni include Jon Silkin, Ken Smith, Tony Harrison, Jeffrey Wainwright, Ian Duhig and Linda France. Its Professor of Poetry is the Poet Laureate Simon Armitage. The University was ground-breaking in its inauguration of Gregory Fellows in the 1950s and among these the poets were James Kirkup, John Heath-Stubbs, Thomas Blackburn, Jon Silkin, William Price Turner, Peter Redgrove, David Wright, Martin Bell, Pearse Hutchinson, Wayne Brown, Kevin Crossley-Holland and Paul Mills. The office of the international quarterly magazine Stand is located on campus. As a result, the poetry archives in the Brotherton Library are among the most extensive and valuable in the UK. More recently, the Academy of Cultural Fellows has included Douglas Caster Fellows Helen Mort, Malika Booker, Vahni Capildeo and Zaffar Kunial. The Leeds University Poetry Centre offers a dynamic resource for research, teaching, and public engagement by supporting and advancing the study of poetry both within and outside the University. It provides a focus for collaborative, interdisciplinary and individual research as well as offering a point of contact for the wider community to share in a range of activities, including readings, workshops, lectures and exhibitions.

The Poetry Centre works closely with the Brotherton Library whose literary collections are of international distinction. All four seventeenth-century Shakespeare folios sit alongside first editions and archival material relating to some of our most celebrated authors and playwrights including Ben Jonson, Charlotte and Emily Brontë and their brother Branwell, Elizabeth Gaskell, Charles Dickens, Evelyn Waugh and others. Our collections relating to living authors are outstanding and include the archive of our Professor of Poetry. The Brotherton's reputation as a major research library is underpinned by the financial endowments left by its founder, Edward Allen Brotherton, 1st Baron Brotherton (1856–1930). The Library continues to enjoy a close relationship with the Brotherton family and we were delighted when the trustees of the Charles Brotherton Trust agreed to support a prize to encourage talented poets who have yet to publish a complete collection. This financial support has enabled the publication of this anthology. We are hugely grateful.

WINNER

Dane Holt is currently completing a PhD at Queen's University, Belfast. His poems have appeared in *Open Ear* and *The Tangerine*. In 2018 he was selected as part of the *Poetry Ireland* Introduction Series.

SHORTLISTED

Pete Green is a poet and musician who grew up in Grimsby and lives in Sheffield. Their debut pamphlet *Sheffield Almanac* was published by Longbarrow Press in 2017. Pete's poetry has also appeared in journals including *Under the Radar*, *Ink Sweat and Tears*, *The Fenland Reed* and *The Interpreter's House*.

Maeve Henry was born in Dublin and lives in Oxford. She holds a Masters in Creative Writing from Oxford Brookes, and her poetry has been widely published. She was recently longlisted for the Live Canon Pamphlet Competition, and was shortlisted for the Wasafiri New Writing Prize in 2018. She is currently completing a novel about a miracle.

Majella Kelly is from Tuam in the West of Ireland. She holds a Masters in Creative Writing from the University of Oxford and has a pamphlet forthcoming in February 2020 with Ignition Press. You can read more at majellakelly.com.

Robyn Maree Pickens is an art writer and poet from Aotearoa/ New Zealand. She is a PhD candidate in ecological aesthetics at the University of Otago, Dunedin.

INTRODUCTION
by Simon Armitage

There is a feeling sometimes that the values of prize-giving and the values of poetry are somewhat incompatible. A prize, by definition, often ends up associating itself with hierarchy, or at least with a form of meritocracy, whereas poetry tends to think of itself, or at least tries to portray itself, as a democratising activity, with ideals of equality and impartiality often informing its commentaries and providing its subject matter. And this is without mentioning the unspeakable topic of financial incentive. Apologies, then, if we offended the sensibilities of the winners of the inaugural Brotherton Prize at the University of Leeds by singling them out for praise and reward. It's true of course that when we sat down to plan the prize we realised we would be making distinctions between poems, and that we would enjoy some entries more than others, and indeed would choose an outright winner. But we also wanted to place an emphasis on consistency, continuity, and development. Hence the Brotherton Prize is one that looks for achievement over a group of poems rather than a single entry, and recognises the page as an exciting and important location for poetry, and seeks to offer guidance, support and editorship as part of its remit. I can only assume from the very high number of submissions we received that a great many poets felt a bond of kinship with those principles, and from the standard of submissions I think those of us involved in originating and organising the prize can feel confident about its shape and design.

Poetry, it seems to me, is in a state of transition at present, adapting to a fast-changing world and coming to terms with revolutions in methods of communication and transmission. Evidence of this transition comes to us in the highly varied styles of contemporary work to be found in both magazines and published books, suggesting that there is no absolute standard of achievement and no agreed consensus of approach. Speech-based poetry, song-based poetry and stage-based poetry are now just as likely to be acknowledged and affirmed as more page-oriented versions of the art, and even within 'literary' poetry a reader can expect to encounter anything from the avant-garde or experimental end of the spectrum to more traditional-looking and conventional-sounding verse, sometimes within the same poem. The plurality and assortment is exciting; it allows for a multiplicity of poetic tones, challenges casually or conveniently held positions, and indicates a degree of inclusiveness and diversity that poetry hasn't always been famous for. It also implies a degree of instability or anxiety about what exactly constitutes a poem: has the word poetry ever held such a wide definition or been so hotly contested? My own response is to embrace the challenge brought about by technological and social change by looking for excellence in each and every poetic method. Put crudely, I'm only interested in work that is capable of saying something about life AND about language, and if that sounds like a fairly modest requirement, it's surprising how often a poem that succeeds on one of those fronts usually fails on the other.

The poems gathered here don't necessarily exemplify the kind of stylistic extremes I've been describing but there's more than enough variation and difference on display to demonstrate the point. And to say something about the wide-ranging tastes of the judges, as well. Pete Green's poems combine an environmental and at times pastoral sensibility with a lyrical dexterity that can include rhyme and pattern, but there's also a mischievousness and irony at play in the fragmented thoughts and the magnified imagery to prove Green is a poet alive to the challenges of the post-modernist era. Maeve Henry's work is instantly publically engaged, but at the level of determined compassion through her detailing of small moments and the particularities of human interaction, not just in its sympathetic documentation of a disordered and unjust system. Her sequence of poetic witnessing reads as a kind of verse-drama at times as she voices her concerns through the controlled framing of tense and intimate situations. Majella Kelly's work is no less concerned with the fate of people and peoples, but has a more ruminative and enigmatic quality; she is a poet of the sensed and the sensual. Ritual, cultural tradition, and the subconscious bring powerful energies to lines and sentences that flirt with the everyday while connecting to deeper and occasionally darker histories. Robyn Maree Pickens writes a flexing and flowing poetry, unpredictable and daring at times, one that can shape-shift from a bold and abrupt comparison ('a sea-urchin that looks like a vagina') or a reference to Grindr, to something far more elusive and elliptical, as in the opening lines of *The time has come for you to lip sync* where she observes:

> Here you are – pulling another foal out of the Ice Age
> as the moon files its tongue down to a shimmer.

The poems are mesmerising and memorable, trippy but never blurred or vague. And Dane Holt, our overall winner, finds poetic significance and literary purchase in the kitchen-sink settings of the commonplace and the everyday. Urban and non-metropolitan poetic forebears such as Ciaran Carson and Tony Harrison can be heard among the echoes of Holt's voice as he encounters High-Court Enforcement Agents and Sheffield Wednesday fans (like 'two soviet tanks'), but enough of his personal idiolect and vernacular confidence is apparent to suggest that this is a poet who is already growing beyond the reach and call of his influences.

Here at the University of Leeds Poetry Centre we warmly congratulate the winners, take great pride in presenting their poems to new readers in published form, and look forward to future editions of the Prize.

Simon Armitage

BROTHERTON POETRY PRIZE ANTHOLOGY

DANE HOLT

REDUNDANCY

is not the end of the world,
is the consensus from the kitchen table.
And another thing: working with his hands

did *his* dad no harm. This last assertion
he knows to be false, but he keeps quiet.
I hadn't heard him swear in the house before

but he called the bailiffs
'bastards', then, 'cunts'. I laughed,
more out of shock than anything,

and caught a slap across the face.
All of a Sunday, he stood by the window
and watched the wind send his dustbin flying.

CAN'T PAY? WE'LL TAKE IT AWAY!

They arrive in vans,
professionalised and civil.
They are 'High-Court Enforcement Agents'
(not 'bailiffs' and *never* 'debt-collectors')
serving letter-headed paperwork on behalf of clients,
wearing bodycams for your,
as well as their, protection;
meanwhile, Paul's cracking jokes back at HQ
with Steve, who's favourite film is *The Dark Knight Rises*,
his favourite meal, lasagne.
Mostly though, they're sympathetic,
and after the initial histrionics
are more than willing to listen
to stories they've heard a million times:
stories of denial, of failing businesses, of things
snowballing, of where the father is
or what country you came from originally.
Once the debt is paid
or goods seized to the value of,
there are no hard feelings,
there are handshakes,
there is universal agreement
that these boys are only doing their job,
and the debtors are left
feeling grateful
for the peaceful entry made into their lives.

VIA SHENANIGANS

We drank enough that night
to paint the Mona Lisa.
We were numbing ourselves,

and if that failed,
killing time until something happened.
And then it did. Afterwards

two Soviet tanks
disguised as Sheffield Wednesday fans
debated who felt more aggrieved

when the girl from earlier
tapped me on the shoulder, whispering
she could roll a joint in thirty seconds flat.

DON'T STIR

It's clear he understands everything
but give him an inch and he'll take a week.
Who says it can't be as simple

as rolling a fat cigar
back and forth between bruised lips?
He's heard the sob stories

from landlords and bailiffs alike,
considers their faces pressed to the window
the dull portraits of a dull century.

They could dismantle this house around him
brick by bastard brick
and he'd sit there like a spoon and not stir.

THOMAS MÜLLER
the Raumdeuter – '*space investigator*'

Perimeters hung with the *feilamort*
of his brother's pelts
        do not deter him. Signs he notes
        on each stretched nerve, along each breath.

Fox-quick, fox-slow, manoeuvring ambuscade
and stout defender's
        boot. He trails his shadow, shedding
        his secrets – useless now – like snake

skin, lizard tail. Never the same route twice;
but finds the same mark.
        The sentries slipped; trap untriggered.
        Chicken-wire clipped; the coop sacked.

Better to catch the breeze in your pocket
or grapple smoke, than
        hope to catch him, seamless through
        traffic, inventing daylight.

A STEP FORWARD

Impressive £10m works to repair and restore New Bolsover Model Village have moved a step forward
– Derbyshire Times, *1 September 2016*

The residents of Villas Road are house proud.
Proud of homes once thought modish real estate,
if only because paid off. And we must respect them.
We must not move them until they are ready.
One afternoon, the ambulance will idle on the kerb

like a taxi. We must understand that many will die here
at home, discovered by next door's neighbourly
curiosity, and concerned proprietors of corner shops.
They shall be carried out, relieved of single beds,
stagnant baths, and we must appreciate that their greyness

is a kind of pride – foreign to us –
in dying just where they'd always lived.
On lawns, a stewardship of cats keep watch
as grown-up children with grandchildren come
like the first ideas of rain, followed by the rain.

THE HOPE FOR US ALL

Our Granddad is raving about his German
shampoo, which has yielded, to date, 47
new hairs, which is, he tells us, pulling
from his back pocket his wife's red-leather,
repurposed address book, a growth-rate of
15.67 hairs a week, 2.22 hairs a day,
0.0925 hairs an hour.
By his calculations, this time next year
he'll have grown 814.14 hairs.
The average human scalp contains
around 100,000 hair follicles,
though he refuses to get ahead of himself.
Even so, in this small turn of events there is
hope for us all, he concludes over dinner,
wearing his best suit – the one put aside
for a wedding and two funerals – a small
comb tucked in his breast pocket,
looking 10 years younger, at least.

‘WHY BACK FROM THE SKY?’

When the topic of death was broached
by their four-year-old daughter, they chose

a robin as their belief, their brief
understandable. Now, this winter

she points and proudly announces
‘There’s Grandma!’ She pauses, then,

and asks, ‘Why back from the sky?’

OUR HOUSE

This paper will soon
yellow, but what you make is fresh.
Our house
you tell us. Your style
frightens – the fear of something lost
in us:

your untrained brutal
lines fidgeting to outgrow this
template;
the crude happy stick-
people coloured sky-blue like the
sky; the

impossible cow,
purple and greater than a green
moon; signed
POPPY with a blood-
orange swipe. Unseasonable
sun. Warmth.

ANDREA PIRLO
Regista – '*the director*'

The academy admired his *monde dramatique*:
the various weight lent to light and to shadow,
the containment of fields, the scope of an attic;
but were moved most of all by his *tactique*
of realism: real horses, real men, live ammo.

CHRISTMAS EVE

I took the underdog at 9/2.
A good price, considering the favourite
was three pints deeper to my eye.

Though as for that, the whiskey
had them really about the same.
Truly, there was little between them

but a length of scar
one had dealt the other
the last time they'd faced off –

the full weight of history in their respective corners
in the form of their respective fathers,
being half-brothers.

PETE GREEN

A CHERRY TREE IN APRIL

Eleven months of ruggedness are
so much grey pretence. Oak is
not the only tree

so spare these bruising lenticels
all that is boisterous,
let us ditch

arboreal clichés of fortitude, shrug aside
statuesque machismo
that I may

transition into springtime with
insouciant pizazz
to ripple and relinquish

these ticker-tape pinks,
adolescent bridesmaid
adorning a breeze;

let breathless fritillaries
fangirl each lush inflorescence,
fulfilling the lilac identity

May fritters away to the roadside,
June denudes us of.
Remember me like this:

not taciturn and shrinking, stoic, sapless,
not abiding the doltish
brunt of boot and clamber,

but as I bear my self,
unabashed of silken prettiness
in April's scantest aperture.

THE WHEEL

Before leaving Pittsburgh we would have asked God to bless
your Nissan. It may have been the day we walked downtown
where the Ohio River becomes greater than the sum
of the Allegheny and Monongahela. I'm guessing we picked up
Interstate 77 just past MacArthur, West Virginia and the mint
gold receding hills you parked up to show me were the Jefferson
National Forest. I remember signs for Roanoke, the name
caught like a strange song. I suspect there remained
a Clinton/Gore sticker on your windscreen, windshield,
whatever. Each time we returned to the car I forgot where I was,
dreamwalked round the wrong side, drunk on love and jetlag.
Oh, you wanna drive? you teased, knowing I'd never even
taken a lesson. When it happened we were zooming into
a crimson sun on a swansong, so maybe that southwestern sweep
just short of the state line and North Carolina. The finer detail
of being 21 rests in stasis, like data on a three-inch floppy disk,
unerased but unretrievable. Next time you pray, pray that I recover
those ten illuminated seconds when some surging confluence
of faith and youth possessed me to agree and hold the wheel
at 70mph so you could tie your hair back without stopping.

ELEGY FOR LE GRAND K

Open the vault
with infinite care,
raise the dome
of polished glass
for a final time:
one false move
may sink satellites,
unravel nanotech.
A century like this
calls for steadiness.

This stolid cylinder
carried the weight
of the world,
casketed regally
against small decay,
its fretful, velvet-
gloved attendants
vexed by the
negligible creep of
discrepancy.

The urge is strong
to place a palm,
absorb the balm
of its assuredness,
allow the gleam
of the Supreme

Kilogram's definitive
iridium to soothe
post-truth disquiet,
smooth out doubt.

Its electromagnetic
successor may not
embody decimal
perfectibility
but twenty atoms
are amiss. Drink
a toast to the K
of precisely one litre,
its desuetude
a subdued *au revoir*
to the palpable.

POET'S NOTE: *'Le Grand K' is the nickname given to the object used to define the mass of a kilogram from 1889 to 2019. Fabricated from platinum and iridium, and officially named the International Prototype of the Kilogram, it was kept in a secure vault in Paris. It was superseded by a measure based on the Planck constant, a value related to the electromagnetic action of photons and thus hard-wired into the fabric of the universe.*

MY HEART IS NOT IAMBIC

My heart is not iambic
My heart was reverse engineered from a mapping by transthoracic echocardiogram, yielding the blueprints for sonic cathedrals
My heart is not iambic, nor spondaic, nor the pedestrian drummer who plods the terrains of mid-tempo with a landfill indie band
My heart is sometimes dactylic with episodes of paroxysmal sprung rhythm
My heart improvises interludes in awkward times, 5/4, 9/8
My heart knows the grand insurmountable force of the notes you don't play, of the beats that it skips, of white space on a page, of mutual deterrence
My heart is a concept album about brinkmanship
My heart tends to improvise lengthy meandering solos remembering kisses averted by ice-cool disposal squads snipping through the correct artery with three seconds remaining on the timer
My heart still extrapolates four hypothetical lovers from out of the time-effaced memory of those averted kisses
My heart has a GPS tracker which faithfully relays its roving data to my hypothetical lovers
My heart is revealed by the tracker at moments of orgasm, D chord, and total eclipse to be located simultaneously everywhere and nowhere
My heart is awaiting the leaving of my hypothetical lovers, allowing its status to switch to unknown, simultaneously beating and not beating
My heart is Schrodinger's heart
My heart did not chart
My heart is the makeshift device that failed to detonate but is yet to be made safe

My heart is not iambic
My heart's frequent flare-ups of narrow complex tachycardia aim
  to articulate some of the many anxieties of a fibrillating world
My heart notes the way Ernest Rutherford's work split the atom
  and aims to apply the same principles to itself, to your name,
  to common sense, to split the morpheme
My heart's diffident rhythm is fixed by the faltering tick of the
  dissident bomb that forgot the script and slumbered forlorn
  in an Audi Coupé during my blowout in a bar 50 metres away
My heart's twitchy syncopation is chiefly dictated by Article 50
  and Hurricane Katrina
My heart rate reflects fluctuations in staffing of libraries and the
  declining extent of polar bear territory
My heart takes the point that unemphasised syllables echo the
  stressed beats to come but sinkholes in Florida issue no terse
  coded warning before ingesting a laundromat
My heart rejects regular metre and classic fixed forms on the
  basis that both constitute a poetic and cardiological fallacy
  during a week that sees mustard gas cascade on Damascus
  and the Duchess of Sussex close a car door
My heart may have once been iambic but not since it marked
  the chaotic dispersion of billowing rubble and dust from the
  asymmetrical collapse of the towers
My heart acts on feedback from specialists finding no special
  affinity threading a rock-steady narrative *ba-dum ba-dum*
  ba-dum through a midnight flurry of knives in backstreet
  Hackney
My heart has been scanned under sterile conditions by
  prominent figures in cultural studies and diagnosed as post-
  ironic with high risk of becoming post-post-ironic

My heart is not iambic
My heart was once schooled in strict rhyming tetrameter pairs
  by a time-serving teacher detesting all poetry, children or

both, and predictably it took a wayward turn
My heart pauses frequently, giving your heart ample time to
confirm understanding or challenge the presuppositions
underlying its most recent beat
My heart is the one who asks unneeded questions as seminars
draw to a close, thus incurring the fury of delegates by delaying
the break for coffee
My heart has no integral memory and strongly objects to the use
of the phrase 'off by heart' to denote something learned
My heart is the opposite of autocorrect
My heart is an obsolete means of encryption
My heart is making landfall over Gulfport, Mississippi
My heart suspends its business so that summits can conclude
negotiations and sign off important treaties between beats
My heart looked on passively as the space between its beats was
declared *terra nullius* by a speculative group of internet cranks
who proceeded to colonise the space and found a micronation
My heart then evicted the settlers by beating at 149 bpm
My heart leaves its beating to one day before a tough deadline
and then pulls an all-nighter
My heart is not teetotal
My heart is basically trolling me
My heart is appalled by its own timidity
My heart's staccato signature is as distinctive as a fingerprint and
will betray me to the authorities
My heart's latest plot was uncovered by squads of elite
cardiologists fixing electrodes to my trembling skin and
monitoring its suspicious activity for 48 hours
When they flicked a switch the screen montaged through ones
and zeroes, nanobots, flash floods, tap water run through with
trihalomethanes and lead, convulsing commodity markets,
the planet's dwindling lithium deposits, zeroes, trenches of
flame stacked with oranges covered in kerosene then set
ablaze to protect wholesale value, ones and zeroes, a soundless

Nuremberg rally with a million blank faces in headphones,
zeroes, barcode tattoos, 3D-printed handguns, a human
resources boss contemplating subcutaneous microchip
implants to monitor staff, flatlining commodity markets,
quantum foam, grey goo, the whole world swiping left

CURLEWS

On a failing clifftop path
you halt and hush me,
pull out from the ice-flecked air
sad and steady minims
fluting through a perfect fifth.

This is their call. Curlews
glissando the headland
cluttered by gulls,
riding out the crisis
on soft thermals of aplomb.

Love, let's take some notes.

THE ABSENCES*

This scene. A playground in a suburb,
rainswept, nameless; a populace
implicit in the empty swing's
small restlessness. Here is Wednesday
afternoon. The path takes off

beyond drenched banks of
privet, flowerbeds clipped circular,
the glade above the cemetery
where Subway wrappers
missed the bin. Somewhere else

is where the soundtrack starts:
three streets away a builder's truck,
its empty flatbed's jolt and clank.
Assume its wipers' bland
defiance. On the adjacent corner

a salon's solitary client may
discreetly lick a fingertip
to riffle magazine pages,
yawning below the blowdry.
Her ringtone perhaps coincides

with the intervention of
a bell releasing scrums of pent-up
pupils and their performed bluster.
Headlights will sweep
the first shadings of dusk

but all of that is elsewhere
and to come. Instead zoom in –
a poplar leaf relinquishes
a single droplet with the seasoned
hand of a Speyside connoisseur

which slaloms down the frame
cradling the swings, negotiates
angular graffiti scratched into the
decades, each layer a trend, a rise
and fall, a sea-change, a regime.

---

* *'The Absences' was first published in issue 7 of* The Fenland Reed.

FAR NORTH LINE*

When I go north I learn of scale, of continuity.
There's always further left to go. A saltire
whips above a shed, like a five-bar gate swinging
open in a storm. This is Brora: scantness,
dauntless, a moment of the world

leaning in. Trampoline children hang
in the air, grin at the train, spread fingertips scribing
curves through sparse atmosphere.
One grey, folded man counts
down days from a speck of a bungalow.

This line's an exercise, this trip a practice of
absurd immersions. Emptiness is
exponential. 'How are we going to get back?'
you beam, necking more Jura. A perching heron
pleases you. A girl is old enough

to graze a horse alone by breaking waves,
young enough to wave up
at our approach to Helmsdale. Somewhere
it's Saturday afternoon, somewhere
our kids scoff cake. Forty miles more of Caithness

emptiness await. How are we going to get back?

---

* *'Far North Line' was first published in issue 66 of* The Interpreter's House.

POSTCARD FROM A STAFF AWAY DAY

I'm writing this outside the Holiday Inn
while the coffee and the river flow. A fire
        escape, a plaque to commemorate
the station closed in 1970. My last boss
but one, the one I liked, stepped out to chat
and pointed out a platform's concrete lip.
        We riffed on how landscapes outlive
the reasons that reshape them, and the way
a dead-end viaduct, disremembered on a
city centre's undrawn boundary, becomes
        lonelier than anywhere.

Inside a hundred admin staff, marketers
and middle managers have broken off
        into small groups to stockpile
abstract nouns against austerity. This is now
        a time of great upheaval in the
landscape for our sector. Holding to our
values is the key to managing change.
        The posh facilitator once drove
round and round a roundabout in tears.
Her Powerpoint roadmapped the warning signs
        of unresolved transition.

Wish you were here. All that makes
sense today are the gold hypothetical
thread your steps narrate about the city
divining great upheaval in the landscape
        and the flicker of your eyes
as we watch decades tumble through a weir.
        We would break off
for a listening process with the River Don,
        brainstorm with kingfishers,
        work in a pair to understand
our own responses to the changing
densenesses of reedbeds. We would
negotiate with dragonflies our action plan
        to leave things as they are.

MAEVE HENRY

RECEPTION

Our cell, you write, smells of spunk
and dirty flip flops. Maybe I'll tell you

how the reception reeks of sour coffee,
how the guard doesn't want to let me

in. She frowns at my foreign passport,
turns my gas bill this way and that,

checks the spelling of my name on her
list, disappointed there is no mistake.

Her face lights up when I show her
the poetry book I have brought you;

another thing to be patted down,
searched for hidden meanings,

misread. *Look this way for the camera,*
put your finger in the scanner, she says.

I smile. She has no smile, not for me.
that would be to admit we are people

caught in a situation. *Put your bag*
in a locker. Not any locker. That one.

Bang it hard, then you can turn the key
I think of the noise of keys, how, later,

as they are locking you up, I will lock
myself into our flat, turning deadbolt

and spring lock, putting on the chain.

VISITORS' ROOM

Two yellow lines across the yard, my feet
inside them. What will happen if I break

out of the lines? Thin men in dark blue
sweats lounge against the walls, palms

guarding cigarettes. Slices of cheap white
bread are folded into their pockets for the

hunger after lockup. They stare like I am
meat on a barbecue, succulent and hot

and the fat white guard in his private army
uniform, my escort, gives them a wink.

Everyone in detention, you write, has a life
hidden from his case owner, the sound

of his mother's voice singing in the kitchen,
the way the light fell on the street where he

grew up. How home tightened in his throat
or was scored into his skin - unprovable.

Fear is not evidence. Scars are not
evidence. The broken kaleidoscope

of a mind that cannot retrieve dates
and times is *de facto* not evidence.

We reach the door. The guard pulls up
his chain and its ball of metal mistletoe

and the key slides into the lock.

IMAGINE A WEDDING

At home I have a photograph of my parents
tying the knot in Kodachrome. Outside the

church men with drums, and clarinets
are waiting to lead them and their guests

to a hotel reception where there will be
mezza and arak, dancing and speeches.

My mother in her white veil, my father in his
new suit, smile into the sun. Wedding rings

they wear for thirty years will be sold for bread,
the clarinettists will be hanged. The future

hidden inside that photograph, the rubble
of Mosul, the church blown up, the Gate of God

destroyed. Last spring they were alive, and now
they are dust. Imagine our wedding, you say

taking my hand across the table. Imagine
they let me out. It could happen. Miracles

follow faith. Your eyes have dark bruises
under them. You haven't slept, you are drunk

on dreams, your passport found, your asylum
case approved, your removal date - set out

in their letter – cancelled. *An emergency travel*
document has been obtained. Your flight to

Rome, habibi, is in three days.

A FINGERPRINT IN ITALY

God will help me, you wrote from Izmir
after the months of silence. You risked

the sea crossing to Lesbos. A thousand
dollars for a seat in a smuggler's boat

that broke up in the shallows off the Turkish
coast. Nights sleeping in the open with

the other pilgrims. A thousand dollars risked
again. This time the boat breaks up in

Greek waters; you swim to land, walk miles
to the refuge. The story you tell so lightly,

forgetting the cameras beaming out pictures of
the drowned and the abandoned whom God

did not help. I slept beside you for months,
when you finally arrived. I know why you

scream in your sleep. Lesbos to Patras.
From Patras across to Bari, where you fell

into the hands of thieves. Beaten, penniless,
picked up by the police. Fingerprints taken.

You walked from the port to the Basilica
di San Nicola. Prayed in front of his relics.

Then came, you say, a miracle of kindness.
A lorry driver on the slip road beckoned you

fetched you a thousand miles closer to me.

THE JUNGLE

The law of the jungle was signed in Dublin.
It's a game the rich countries play against

the poor ones. Send them back, it's called,
find the fingerprint. Imagine the millions

of fingerprints of migrants, touching the sides
of the boats, the sides of the lorries, pressed

down into ink in police stations across Europe.
And yours, in Bari. No matter how long you

crouched under plastic in Calais, no matter
how long you slept beside me in the flat,

your fingerprints are recorded in Italy. Italy will
decide. I take your hand, turn it palm upward.

trace its life line, kiss each betraying fingertip.
In my head is the noise of engines taking off

so loud it silences speech. What can we say
to each other, in this room, in front of guards?

Hands locked. Unlocked. I get up, I step away.
Keys open the door to the outside, the yellow

lines, the lounging men, a sky criss-crossed by
vapour trails. The roaring in my head increases

as the woman in reception laughs with the guard.
Shall I tell you they are laughing at my head scarf,

how she smiles as she unlocks the exit door?
No, habibi. None of it matters any more.

BIRD-SPOTTING IN PALMYRA*

It wasn't a crow. We'd shot the crows already,
hung them on posts as a warning to the starlings.
No, this was exotic; wings as big as a flag
and an old bald head, reddened by many summers.
Yusaf caught it flapping around the temple precinct,
ugly and helpless, with a high, hoarse cry under torture,
but it told us nothing useful. Ahmed put a sign
round its neck and we strung it with red twine
from the traffic lights. The photograph I posted
from my phone went viral. Ten thousand likes.
Tomorrow when the power comes back on
we're electrifying a net across the sky. No spring
migration this year for the starlings, no murmuration.

It was a bald ibis, according to Google. One of a handful left.

---

* *'Birdspotting in Palmyra' was first published in* Ver Poets Prize Anthology 2016.

SOMEONE ELSE*

The quilt still smells of you, but your bedroom walls
are pocked with blu-tack, football teams all gone.
They say you crossed the border, walked into Syria.
You will head home, I tell them. As you used to
come back from parties, drunk on girls and spliffs.
You will come in, yawning, lifting the lids
of my saucepans, grabbing a spoon. I will say,
your father is worried. Why are you breaking my heart?

It's done. It's broken. I was looking the wrong way,
like the guards at the airport. They caught you on camera,
clear as the scan of my womb. Now someone else
is being born, a boy with a gun, screaming obscenities.
And the view from your room is just the same:
that lilac bush, a blackbird, the washing line.

---

* *'Someone Else' was first published on* Poets and Players *website summer 2015.*

CHECKPOINT*

You can see a red line where our country ends.
On one side, pumpkins and graves. On the other,
the future. The guards are checking cars for smuggled
goods. We have hidden our memories in Granddad,
who looks so innocent, so confused –

a single rough word startles him into tears.
He sits upright in the middle of the back seat
packed round with children, keeping his hand
clamped over the mouth of the littlest one,
who knows all the songs.

---

* *'Checkpoint' was first published in* The North *2017 (Wordsworth Trust Prize).*

MAJELLA KELLY

'If you come here you'll find no mass grave, no evidence that children were ever so buried, and a local police force casting their eyes to heaven and saying 'Yeah, a few bones were found – but this was an area where famine victims were buried. So?"

— The Bon Secours religious order, via a PR consultant, in response to juvenile human remains at Tuam's former Mother and Baby Home.

THE SEVENTH ACRE

A memorial garden squats on a small parcel
of land behind a row of houses like a Síle
-na-Gig hunkered and holding her genitals
open like two halves of an apple. A ruminant
garden, her belly's distended by numerous
stomachs. If you come here you'll find her
chewing her cud, coughing up a mandible
perhaps, or an ankle, spitting out tiny pips
of spinal column. Somebody saw a small boy
once running across her shorn scalp rattling
a skull on a stick. For this is the seventh acre,
the acre that ate babies, but only the ones
whose mothers were sinners, ones it was right
to leave nightly rocking themselves to sleep.

SKULL ON A STICK

A young boy runs across the grass rattling
a skull on a stick. The skull has a near-
perfect set of teeth and it bursts out laughing
when it catches sight of them in the wing
mirror of a parked Ford Cortina. The more
the skull in the mirror laughs, the more the skull
on the stick laughs back, unaware it's laughing
at itself. *Are you my mother?* the skull
says to its reflection. Then the boy races
through the bishop's spacious and well-kept Palace
grounds. *Daddy!* the skull blurts after a spurt
of purple ushered hurriedly into its large
and handsome mansion. Until the boy's mother
puts her head out an upstairs window yelling:
Put that thing back where you found it this minute,
Martin, and get in here for your dinner.
The skull doesn't understand, but it smiles
widely with its near-perfect set of teeth.

CRAB-APPLE

This particular tree is legitimate.
Deliberately grown, it's not one of those
misbegotten lot that grew true from a pip
dropped by a waxwing or a blackbird
in a forest or a hedgerow. In autumn
its harvest was precious, each crab-apple
fondly thumbed like a bead of a rosary,
a jewel treasured for pies and jellies.

But the garden where it was originally
planted got neglected. Next to an ancient
septic tank, this once noble, now ruffian,
of the woods withered to skin and bone,
leaves puckered, twigs curled into Shepherds'
crooks. There was something not quite clean
about it, cankers on its bark oozing
a cloudy liquid in cold damp weather

like the snot-filled noses of children
with no one to care for them. Then one year
the crop was left to rot in the grass.
The loss of the sweet pink jam on the tongues
of the nuns come winter was briefly grieved
but by and by the gravity of the fall of one
small and sour fruit was comparable
to one more baby born out of wedlock.

THERE GO I

Everyone turned to stare when the hare turned
up at the back of the church like a twitching
bride ready to walk up the aisle. Of course
a hare can't walk exactly, for no matter
how slowly she moves among the mangel-
wurzels or the oilseed rape, she looks ungainly.
A hare has no interest in marriage either
since she likes to be promiscuous, doesn't
care that some would call her leverets *bastards*
by different fathers. And regardless of
how many times her nest gets trodden on,
she'd never call it *broken*. Nor does she feel
she's failed at life. On the contrary, like the day
you were born, furred, your eyes wide open.

SKULL IN THE SAND

One morning the tide drops a skull at my feet.
A handful of small shells roly-poly

from its nose-holes, strands of seaweed fan
about its empty head and the sea foams

from its open mouth like a muffled conversation
about drowning. Instead of reburying it

I place it in the crook of some rocks
so the cliffs might cradle it and the sea sing

it ancient songs of wild salmon searching
for the scent of their home river.

At first the wind wallops through the eye-
sockets with all its hollow impossible thoughts.

But soon the skull is heady with the smell
of wild mint and heather, not to mention

the small-talk of a wren. Before long it is jammers
with twigs and moss and feathers

and the only thing on its mind by spring
are five perfect white eggs with red speckles.

VIRGINIA CREEPER
talking to a remnant of the boundary wall

Shade makes me aggressive. I twist my hair.
I stare at my fingers. Don't say *oppressor*.
I'm afraid of the dark. When I grip the throats
of those weaker it's not that I want to
choke them. I need to reach your pretty neck
-lace of broken glass. I only cut myself
so you'll love me. Stop saying I'm clingy.
It's not my fault all my thoughts are flawed.
My bootless shoots rooted where they fell and I
fasten myself to you for good reason.
You could be ripped from me while I'm sleeping.
Please. Be my mother. I know my little
green flowers aren't worthy and these blue-black
berries toxic, but in Autumn I'll make
you proud. Watch me set my every leaf ablaze.

OVER-PAINTING

In the same way that Rudolph II
had the babies in Bruegel's *Massacre
of the Innocents* over-painted, so men
from Galway County Council were sent
with spades and grass seeds to lay a lawn
over the septic tank where juvenile
human remains were known to be found.

In the same way the nuns kept insisting
that no children were ever so buried.

In the painting a woman weeps over
an array of cheese and charcuterie
which creates a scene arguably more
resonant of calculated evil;
the absence of blood and gore more eerie
and still than the heinous original.

THE OLD HARE

A hare limps slowly through the deep narrow rooms under the Memorial Garden muttering to herself. She is old and worn out. Her top lip is split and her teeth protrude. *All the goddesses are gone*, she spits. *Banished with the snakes and replaced with saints. Saints! What use are saints down here? And what bloody good were they up there? Saint Gerard Majella, my arse!* The roots of the crab-apple stretch to caress her rough grey pelt. *Be patient*, they tell her, *a new goddess will come, you'll see.*

What did they ever see in Christianity? the old hare continues. *The pagans never named any child 'bastard'. And was it Christian to toss their bodies in an old septic tank such as this like the empty carcass of a chicken, stripped and boiled up for soup?* Hares don't take readily to cages, rabbits being the borrow-loving ones, the ones more likely to let a human cradle them. And yet she stays.

There's a soft thud like a just-shot pheasant and the old hare sits with her ears back listening to the hushed voices above her as they slither along the shadow of the high wall, which bears so lightly its crown of broken glass:

Oh, sister, I feel sorry for the baby. It's still a human being though, isn't it?

That child's mother was ***not*** *married. Understand this,* ***we*** *are in charge of the soul here.*

The old hare rises again shaking her head. She catches the cotton corners of moonlight that peeped through the cracked concrete slab and tucks it under a cold white chin. *Always remember your mother loved you very much,* she reassures the still little bundle, *and that she would've taken you with her if she could.*

At dawn a vigil of robins hover over the makeshift crypt plucking out their own breast feathers so its darkness be silken and tinged with pink. Then ravens, in their black shawls, process solemnly through the brambles bearing forget-me-nots.

CLEAN

Dead is the happiest we ever were.
In life we were the hidden children
of sin. In death sweet gifts
of benediction for a congregation
of insects. How exquisite our decay.
You could say it was a washing
away of wrongs. Clean at last,
our comingled bones were rinsed
of flesh until a halo of moths foraged
softly on every last hair on our heads.

And now we are forget-me-nots, blinking
in the sudden sunshine of an autumn meadow
gone to seed, the cries of small children
catching on the slightest breeze.

FORGET

Forget the Memorial Garden. It doesn't know
what it's supposed to remember. Could it be connected
to the name of the town: Tuaim=tumulus=burial ground?

Never mind. Was it for famine victims when it was a workhouse?
Or soldiers when it was a barracks? Or maybe the Mothers
& Babies when it was their Home? No.

What kind of home has high walls topped with broken glass?
Forget the Memorial Garden. It can't remember its secret underground
chambers once used for sewage, remembers less the seven hundred

and ninety six missing children. All that's on its mind today
is the thrush's nest in the Guelder Rose (which, by the way, knows
it isn't really a rose) and what haunts the garden most

are the blunt ends of the blue-green eggs. Will there be enough
air for the chicks to breathe before they break their shells?

ROBYN MAREE PICKENS

CONTEXT

Isis was a major goddess before she became an acronym
My friend is overwhelmed because he is on Grindr in Spain
One can only compare Krakatoa's newly minted lava with a newborn
in the context of bacteriological study
(both surfaces would soon become colonised with bacteria and growth)

We are salt meadows our lives sometimes in synch with our blooms
We had talked about an internet-free weekend
This was the context
I had come back from a conference talking about durian fruit

We were sitting in two unfamiliar chairs
The sun at our backs and you said draw me a durian
But I couldn't because I hadn't seen one
Later I watched YouTube videos on how to eat a durian

I collected words for you, nice ones I could rub into you like: butter /
custard / avocado / omelette / flan / your pulse /
and words I would quarantine like: organs / innards / rotten pineapple /
spiky / pungent /
I would not give you durian in one hand unless I had mangosteen in the
other

If I raise your temperature (durian) I need to know how to bring it down
again (mangosteen)
Pungent is not so bad and we need our organs
I hear Anthony singing 'grow back like a starfish' in his divine falsetto
and I want the lightness of coral spawning to flow between us always

MOVING IN

You placed the glass jar of seawater next to the framed postcard
of the moon and now I can only see it as a watery planet. This is

how it is when you move in together as a couple. I brought the red
vase closer to another framed postcard—of a yellow Grayson Perry

vase—and together we positioned the carapace of a sea urchin
that looks like a vagina in front of them. I think we should bring back

shrines of our own making. Your aunt found the perfect-sized pink
container to shield the fragile sea vagina as it travelled with you from

Ireland to Aotearoa. Tonight I will say, this is our shrine. You know—
I would become each of the four sons of Horus for you, to guard

your viscera when you pass (in the distant future). I will guard
the four necessary organs—stomach, intestines, lungs, liver. This is

how it is when you move in together. You must learn where the sun
falls to position plants for maximum happiness. You must adjust

to the downstairs cough that rises through the welter, the folx
living in low-rent flats opposite who still burn coal and the singe of it

on your lungs walking home on winter nights and the fat cat who runs
towards you in error. There is so much misdirected, unnoticed love

in spam mail. It is unexpected, like a cluster of monks with Nirvana totes
over their slender shoulders. Modified pollen. I would like to

communication with you. Like when two black horses meet
on a snowy plain. Steam flaring. We have yet to sage our apartment

—remove any distress oxides, left-behind karma, limbo stop-overs,
streaky shadows, unseen thickets. I wonder what we are waiting for?

We also need coasters, stronger light bulbs in most rooms
and another lamp. These are as important as a lizard's tongue, the way

it darts in the dark, all sleek, while flowers rain down. Then there are
the cobwebs—the ones along the top of the sash window that we were

both so sure we'd clear. How could the previous tenant have lived
with them? Yet here we are, a month in. These three—plants, sage,

cobwebs—this temporary failure of hygiene—belong to the same hand.
When we do one, we'll do all three. Like when I become the four sons of Horus

for you I'll transmute—north, south, east, west with exceptional alacrity
to keep your viscera warm and honey combed.

THE TIME HAS COME FOR YOU TO LIP SYNC

Here you are—pulling another foal out of the Ice Age
as the moon files its tongue down to a shimmer. A frog

with a third eye leaps off a white plate & I can still smell
you on my fingers. We sit in the briny shallows with the bony

fish watching icebergs crack and calve with the spontaneity
of my mother's spine. We have tipped sunlight into a kiln

& are left here grinding pearls & fighting over definitions
of tolerable risk. I open your freezer & take out one

of David Hammon's Bliz-aard balls that you bought
from his performance rug on the corner of Cooper Square & Astor Place.

I hold up one palm-rolled compression of snow for you to see.
We remember what it felt like to arrange dancers

& sit bare chested in the dirty rain.

SOMA

Listen like we are just passing through here
on hikers' knees with every strand of light

bending into green breath and leaf cortex between us.
Who has not stood with one foot in torrid

the other in temperate under heavy rain
looking for the clouded leopard amongst slate and shale

a leather patch for unseen grace, the ripe fig
ripped to a gash, palms heavy and dessicant

expecting a blackened ibex skull to sing
while shouldering radiation along your backbone

feeling traces of fire on the cave wall
willing to trade all the ghost money burners

a five-spouted jar in underglaze blue from the Qing dynasty
to lead reindeer to lichen, to suckle Sichuan red earth

to feel the wick inside and set aside the fish oil lamp
to lie next to ancient Antarctic moss

lick fern bulbs into bud and stand together on the edge
pawing at starlight.

AN ERROR HAS OCCURRED

An error has occurred. Please try again later.

Seven goats coasting on the equinoctial tide have disrupted reception.

This is the fifty-third day of rain and we are tired.

I am too absorbed tracing bora trails in floorboards to help you.

The squares of graph paper hurt our eyes.

The fragrance of fig leaves has stolen me away from my console.

I am split with grief like Gordon Matta-Clark; forgive me.

A co-worker has just returned with donuts.

We are watching polar bears forage for food in apartments.

Everywhere ice is melting; I am bereft.

We are watching security footage of a couple having awkward sex.

I was compelled to go outside and walk barefoot on the grass.

Rats have chewed through our industrial-strength cables.

I am listening to one song on repeat and cannot break free.

We're waiting for the new employee to arrive.

The statue of liberty has fallen down.

I am without joy this morning.

An old man with sailor tattoos is staring at us from his balcony.

We have gone to the casino in the desert by the Joshua Tree.

I keep seeing headless heads upside down in a millpond.

The sun has a long threatening tongue today.

The camel has laid its head on the sand and I am hoarse.

We both dreamed of teeth stacked like blue pain.

LONG DISTANCE

You ask me what I would do to stay in contact with you

I say I will be complicit in the mining of rare earth minerals.

(Yttrium, Lanthanum, Cerium, Praseodynium, Neodymium, Europium, Gadolinium, Terbium, Dysprosium.)

I sit in one bundled piece at a turquoise school desk with ice fields cracking around me in a supermarket of light. I miss the antiquarian disassembly of pre-pixel video.

(Indium tin oxide enables me to touch you, Terbium & Dysprosium to see you in rich, heightened colour as if you were here.)

You ask me for a metaphor of 'us'

I offer the fig & the wasp—precision biological mutualism—but no one dies.

We must be together on the same earth island or riding the brow of the king tide between 2020 – 2050 when Dysprosium & the hungry fishes of the ocean run out.

To stay in contact with you I use approximately 62 different types of metals & 16 of the 17 rare earth minerals.

YOUR STRONG NECK

I came to see the moon as a watery planet
but now the glass jar of seawater stands empty in the kitchen

It was time or it dried up
The postcard of the moon is on the other side of the room

You took the red vase (which was yours)
so the framed postcard of a Grayson Perry vase leans alone

Your country was unreachable without you
even as I trooped around all its treasures

I did go to the Archaeology Museum
Saw cauldrons, spirals, lunalae (gold collars of crescentic shape made from thinly beaten gold)

Just now two pairs of birds have flown past against a streaked sky
And the lemons in the fruit bowl (yours) are unpeeling themselves

In your tongue I no longer fit
I weigh sound in angles

I admired the beaten gold necklaces (and loved the description 'pomaceous fruitwood')
but felt closest to a fragment of a woven textile bag

I remember all that it once held and kept together in one place
So dark inside, so secret and tethered

PHARMAKON

In what way are we alive?
    I listen to offers from smoking mouths

Scientifically we are a sequence of protein units
    who form a circle around glucose molecules

Yet we are also seed heads cured by heat
    pungent visionaries ripe for flight

If the secret of creation is hidden in your head
    I take a tincture of Ranunculus for sight

Lie low in my throat now, in this pharmakon of want
    sip fifteen swollen teaspoons of thirst

Let me perch in the trees with the wolves
    and walk on scent in the thick rain

Let me see you down to the bone
    and feel the percussion of your lungs

Sit with me in the taiko corner shining with seed crystals
    as the equinoctial tide canyons into shore

ABOUT THE JUDGES

Simon Armitage was elected Oxford Professor of Poetry from 2015–2019, and in May 2019 was appointed UK Poet Laureate. He has published twelve full-length award-winning collections, most recently *Paper Aeroplane: Selected Poems, 1989-2014* (Faber and Faber, 2014) and *Sandettie Light Vessel Automatic* (Faber and Faber, 2019). His medieval translations include *Sir Gawain and the Green Knight* and *Pearl* which won the 2017 PEN Award for Poetry in Translation. He is a broadcaster, playwright, novelist and the author of three best-selling volumes of non-fiction. Simon Armitage was made CBE for Services to Poetry in 2015 and in 2018 was awarded the Queen's Gold Medal for Poetry. Armitage is Professor of Poetry at the University of Leeds.

Malika Booker is a British Caribbean poet. Her poetry collection *Pepper Seed* (Peepal Tree Press, 2013) was longlisted for the OCM Bocas prize and shortlisted for the Seamus Heaney Centre prize (2014). She is published in *The Penguin Modern Poet Series 3: Your Family: Your Body* (2017). Malika was the Douglas Caster Cultural Fellow at the University of Leeds and is currently a poetry Lecturer at Manchester Metropolitan University.

Melvyn Bragg, Lord Bragg of Wigton, CH, FRS, FBA, FRSL, is an English broadcaster, author and parliamentarian. His novels, mostly set in Cumbria, have won several awards including the John Llewellyn Rhys Prize, WH Smith and Time Life Prizes, and three nominations for The Booker Long list. His non-fiction books include *The Adventure of*

English. He has been Editor and Presenter of *The South Bank Show* since 1978, first on ITV and currently on Sky Arts. In 1988 he began to host *Start The Week* on Radio 4. After his ennoblement in 1998 he moved to present a brand new programme called *In Our Time*, an academic discussion radio programme, which has run to over 800 broadcast editions and has proved to be a strikingly popular global podcast. He was Chancellor of the University of Leeds from 1999 until 2017.

Stella Butler is University Librarian and Keeper of the Brotherton Collection at the University of Leeds. She chairs the panel for the Designation Scheme of Arts Council England which aims to identify and celebrate collections of outstanding significance held in museums, libraries and archives across England. She has published on the history of science and medicine and on libraries and heritage issues.

Trinidadian Scottish writer Vahni Capildeo's seven books and four pamphlets extend from prose poetry into immersive theatre. Their DPhil in Old Norse and translation theory inspires a multi-layered, multilingual approach. Capildeo's work has been honoured by the Cholmondeley Award and the Forward Poetry Prize for Best Collection. They write a regular column for *PN Review*. Capildeo was the Douglas Caster Cultural Fellow in Poetry at the University of Leeds. Their new focus is on the *Odyssey*.

John Whale is the Director of the University of Leeds Poetry Centre. He is the author of two collections of poetry, *Waterloo Teeth* and *Frieze*, both published by Carcanet/Northern House. *Waterloo Teeth* was shortlisted for the Forward Prize's Felix Dennis Prize for best first collection. He is an editor of the international quarterly magazine *Stand*.